Introducing Watercolor Painting

Introducing
Watercolour
Painting

Michael Pope

Book Club Associates
London

© Michael Pope 1973
First published 1973
ISBN 0 7134 2434 6
Reprinted 1974

Filmset by Keyspools Limited
Golborne, Lancashire
Printed in Great Britain at
The Pitman Press, Bath
This edition published by
Book Club Associates
by arrangement with
B T Batsford Limited
4 Fitzhardinge Street, London W1H 0AH

Contents

View of Jerusalem by Edward Lear
The Tate Gallery, London
Pen and watercolour wash drawing obviously a study for an oil
painting as notes are written on the study to remind the artist of
exact details. What 'G's coffee shop' means in the foreground is
anyone's guess, but I suppose it refers to a particular colour

Acknowledgement

My thanks to Adrian Bury who freely gave me
his valuable time and deep experience. To Barry
Evans and Barry Driscoll who both stopped
being busy in order to help me. To Leo Clarke
who did my typing, and to Mr Bown of Lloyds
Bank who did my worrying for me.

The figure above, and figures 22, 27 (copyright
SPADEM Paris), 28, 29, 30, 32, 33, 34, 83, 86, 91
(copyright SPADEM Paris) 92, 93, 94, 95 and 120
are reproduced by kind permission of the
Trustees of The Tate Gallery, London; Figure 96
by kind permission of *Trustees of the Sir John
Soane's Museum, London*.

Colour plate 2 facing page 33 is reproduced by
kind permission of the *Trustees of the Victoria
and Albert Museum, London* and colour plate 3
by kind permission of the *Courtauld Institute
Galleries, London*.

Foreword

The aim of the author is to help the student of painting to extend his knowledge of the techniques and methods of working in watercolour and all the associated media.

The book is not a manual of how to acquire stylistic tricks which will enable the artist to paint the shine on ladies' knees. Explanations of specific painting techniques are only intended to encourage the student to push paint around in different ways.

The quantities of ingredients in the recipes given in the book are expressed in parts by measure (pbm).

Just as there are no steadfast rules for oilpainting, there are none for watercolour either. The rules such as exist are merely those of the limitations of the medium. Oilpaint can be worked over time and time again and each time the top layer of paint will appear fresh, but watercolour requires a lighter, surer touch and the self control to leave ones painting alone before one kills it with overwork.

1 Wooden watercolour box belonging to Adrian Bury filled with hexagonal sticks of architects' watercolour.

2 The palette in use. Note the larger reservoirs for mixing colour washes

Watercolour materials

Colours

The pigments used in the manufacture of water-colours are the same as those used in the manufacture of oil paints, the difference being in the vehicle in which they are bound. Oil paints are generally bound in poppy oil whereas water-colours are bound in gum.

Watercolour paints can be bought in tubes but a more convenient form is in small cakes or pans. Watercolour paint can be made in the studio and it is very satisfying to do so but quite honestly I do not think it is worth the trouble because artist suppliers sell it quite cheaply, and most is of excellent quality.

There is one form of watercolour paint which is sold in hexagonal sticks of colour called *architects' watercolour*. Although there is not a complete range of colours they are of good quality and very economical. (Figure 1.)

Every artist has his own preferences as to the range of colours he uses but it is not necessary to have a vast range.

A good workable palette for me would be:

Yellow ochre	Light red
Raw sienna	Sepia
Burnt sienna	French ultramarine
Gamboge	Cobalt blue
Alizarin crimson	Prussian blue
or Rose madder	Hookers green No. 2

These colours will cover almost any landscape painting the artist may wish to do.

Colour boxes and palettes

Despite the multitude of watercolour boxes and palettes on the market all that is really needed is a simple box big enough to hold the colours, and possibly the brushes, and a palette large enough to hold all the paint needed to be mixed. Such a box is shown in figure 1 and a palette in figure 2.

Figures 3 to 7 show other commercial boxes ranging from cheap and cheerful boxes to serious 'watercolour artist's essential equipment'. I personally carry my colours in a plastic bag and mix my colours on an old tin plate—but I use good quality colours, expensive brushes and the best paper I can afford.

3   A cheap paint box
4   A reasonably adequate paint box
5   A useful box with detachable palette
6   Watercolour palette sold separately
7   Sketching colour box with a water reservoir and container, being used with a quill brush

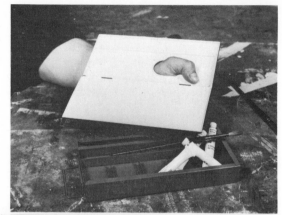

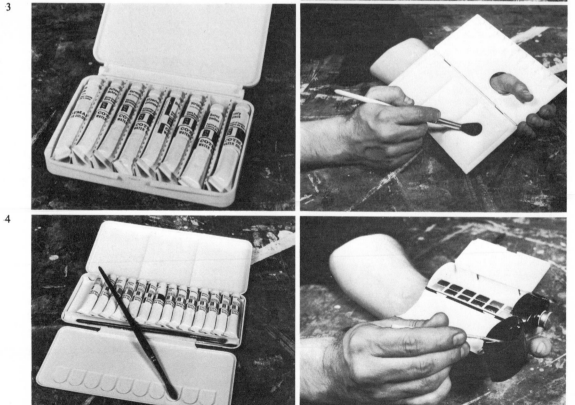

Gouache and designer's colours

There are many opaque watercolours all gum bound and all varying in consistency and permanence. Paints like poster colour and designers' colour are used mainly by designers to lay opaque washes and they have very good covering powers and plenty of 'body'. But check the colourman's list as many colours are not light fast and permanent. Gouache colour has been an accepted paint for many years and can be diluted to transparent washes or used as opaque body colour with equal facility. Do not use it too thickly because, as it dries out, there is a tendency for it to shrink and crack.

Equipment

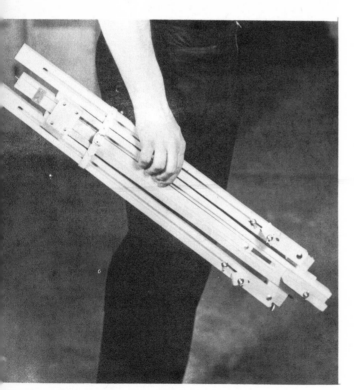

8 Lightweight wooden sketching easel folded for carrying

Easels

When using watercolour in the studio I prefer to work on a bench and when working out of doors I prefer to sit on a stool and rest my drawing board on my lap (figure 12). But many people prefer to stand and paint. For those who do, a collapsible easel is necessary.

There are many on the market, but buy the simplest, sturdiest easel capable of being adjusted to at least three different positions (one of which must be horizontal). The simplest is usually the cheapest. Figures 8 and 9 show just such an easel assembled and folded for carrying.

Stools

Special sketching stools are sold by specialist shops but any store which sells camping gear will be sure to have a range of comfortable lightweight stools. The two requisites of a sketching stool are that it be light to carry and have a seat large enough to carry one comfortably throughout the painting session. It is difficult enough to paint, without having to work under uncomfortable conditions as well. (Figure 10.)

Water carriers

Some colour boxes have built-in reservoirs for carrying water but they never really hold enough and it is necessary to take at least a pint of water out on a sketching expedition. A screw-top plastic bottle is excellent for this. (Figure 1.)

Water containers

An enamelled tin mug is the ideal water container because it is heavy and has a wide base. (Figure 1.) Plastic pots such as yoghurt cartons are generally too light and unstable because the base is smaller than the top.

Bags and satchels

A carrying satchel such as the one illustrated in figure 10, which is sold expressly as a water-colourist's bag, is absolutely fine; it is large enough to take all the equipment *and* a packed lunch.

Drawing boards

In the studio, a drawing board should be as heavy and well made as possible to ensure that it does not warp. But out sketching, weight is a factor to be considered.

No board should be less than 254 mm × 305 mm (10 in. × 12 in.) and how strong it is depends upon the quality of paper to be used. If a very good heavyweight paper is used it can be pinned to the board, as in figure 12, or clipped with drawing board clips, and the painter can be secure in the knowledge that it will not croggle when washes are laid on it.

In order to stretch cheaper paper (see figures 36 to 42) it is necessary to have a board of at least 8-ply wood in order to withstand the tremendous pull of the shrinking paper. Thin ply wood and hardboard are no good at all.

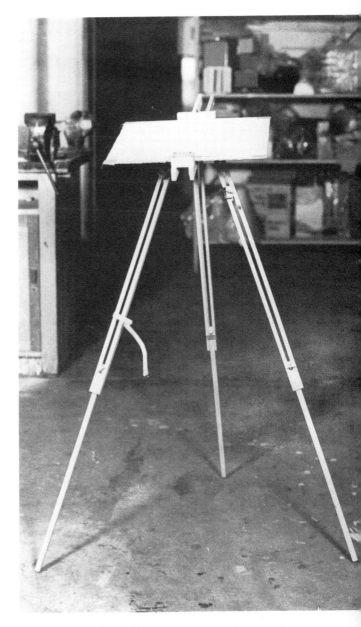

9 Sketching easel assembled ready for painting in watercolours

13

11 A view in Richmond Park, Surrey, chosen as the subject of the watercolour painting by Adrian Bury

10 An artist's satchel containing everything necessary for a day's sketching, except the lightweight aluminium stool which is easy enough to carry

12 Preparing for painting by lightly delineating the limits of the picture with pencil

13 Having indicated the main areas of the composition in pencil, the first thin wash of cobalt blue is laid on the sky. Clouds a mixture of cobalt and light red and beneath the clouds and on the horizon rose madder and yellow ochre

15 The first really decisive mark is made, establishing the tonal relationships to come

14 The skeletal structure of the main trees are indicated preparatory to considering the whole of the middle distance. Tree trunks french blue and burnt sienna. Middle distance hookers green and ultramarine

16 The group of trees in the right middle distance is now firmly painted and becomes a strong tonal mass using prussian blue, burnt sienna and hookers green

15

17 The left-hand side of the picture is painted in and the far and middle distances are firmly established. Hookers green used and some blue painted between groups of trees

19 Some of the more interesting clumps of grass are loosely brushed in to break up the flat expanse of foreground. The painting is virtually finished except for darkening the trees on the right with prussian blue and burnt sienna

18 The painting now extends from the middle distance to the close foreground which is washed in with yellow ochre and alizarin

20 The completed painting

Plate 1 *Richmond Park* by Adrian Bury
The finished painting, slightly strengthened in the studio and put ▶ in a mount

Brushes

The only brushes worth buying are the best quality obtainable. A cheap brush will work well for a couple of months and then start ruining the work whereas a good brush will cost a small fortune initially, but should last a lifetime. The good quality brushes are made of best russian sable, and will possess the following qualities:

1 Ability to hold a wash without flopping.
2 A natural springiness.
3 A shape to which it always returns when dry.
4 It should never shed its hair.

The minimum number one needs are:

Sables: Numbers 16 or 14 round
Numbers 10, 7, 6 and 3 round
Number 12 flat wash

Squirrel—one large wash brush.

Care of brushes

1 Always wash brushes clean after use, preferably under running water because paint left in the brush tends to rot the hair and some paints even react with the metal of the ferrule.

2 Re-form the brush to its original shape after use by spitting in the palm of the hand and twisting and drawing the brush towards the body until a firm point is obtained. A slightly disgusting habit but preferable to putting the brush into the mouth because a number of pigments are relatively poisonous.

3 Store brushes in a box or container so that the hair is not cramped or bent. If the brushes are to be used every day then keep them in a jar on the studio desk, hair upwards.

21   Selection of watercolour brushes

4 Brushes that are going to be stored for a long period of time between use should be kept in a close fitting box with a gew grains of camphor against attacks by a certain type of moth which will decimate them if given the opportunity.

22 *The White House, Chelsea* by Thomas Girtin
The Tate Gallery, London
A pure watercolour painting with large areas of simple wash
heightened by small touches of detailed painting

23 *Landscape with Dedham Church* by Thomas Constable ▶
Typical of Constable's studies for paintings—a direct loose watercolour expressing not only the tonal relationships but also capturing
the atmospheric quality of the moment

24   *Landscape, Capel Curig, North Wales* by Adrian Bury

25   *Landscape* by Adrian Bury ▶
Two watercolours from an artist who has complete control of his medium

26 *In the Fens* by Leopold Rivers
Typical of a certain school of watercolour painting popular during
the Victorian period. Characterised by a stippled fussy technique

27 *They're Biting* by Paul Klee
The Tate Gallery, London
This pen and wash drawing by Paul Klee is a good example of how
he uses the primary quality of watercolour, which is its delicacy
and capacity for infinite nuance, to express his dream world on
paper
Copyright SPADEM, *Paris*

28 *Kirkstall Abbey* by Girtin
A beautifully composed painting of the type of serene landscape which Girtin excelled in
painting

29 *The Seine and the Palace of the Tuileries* by Thomas S. Boys
The Tate Gallery, London
A beautiful painting full of detail drawn with the brush, but some-
how the artist has managed not to overwork his painting and one
of the strongest characteristics of the painting is its lightness

28 *Pale Shelter Scene* by Henry Moore
The Tate Gallery, London
Squared-up drawing in pencil, pen and wash with areas of high-
lights picked out in wax

31 *The Man With The Wooden Leg* by Rowlandson
A characteristic pen and wash drawing where the vigorous flowing
style expresses exactly the bawdy humour of the period

32 *A Married Couple* by George Grosz
The Tate Gallery, London
George Grosz used watercolour as Rowlandson used it, to satirise
and comment on the social conditions of his time. Grosz caught
the feeling and decadence in pre-war Nazi Germany as Rowlandson
expressed the inanities of eighteenth-century life as he saw them.
Grosz used watercolour in a beautifully controlled way

28

33 *The Bright Cloud* by Samuel Palmer
Another example of Palmer's fantastic technique and his ability to
fill a small picture with detail without seemingly to overwork it

34 *The Harvest Moon*
drawing from *A Pastoral Scene* by Samuel Palmer
The Tate Gallery, London
An ink and wash monochromatic drawing full of delights; look at
the richness of the drawing techniques used in one small drawing.
The great romantic watercolourist of all time, in my opinion

35 Pencil and watercolour wash

Paper

Ideally, like brushes, the paper should be of the finest quality. A cheaper quality paper can produce good results if it is first prepared properly by stretching.

The best watercolour paper is hand-made, but this is getting increasingly more difficult to get and a good quality machine-made paper is almost as good. One such as *Green*'s pasteless board 762 mm × 559 mm (200 lb) or a cheaper paper called *Bockingford* are good.

Stretching paper

Any paper other than heavyweight watercolour paper or board has a tendency to croggle when watercolour is applied to it so that it is better to be safe and stretch it before beginning work, than sorry after the painting has been ruined. A fair quality cartridge paper about 110 g per sq. m (60 lb) weight makes a beautiful painting support when stretched

Materials
1 A good drawing board or a piece of marine plywood at least 8-ply.
2 Some brown gummed sticky paper.
3 A piece of rag.
4 A large sink or bath.
5 Paper cut about 15 mm ($\frac{1}{2}$ in.) smaller all round than the board.

Method

1 Cut four pieces of gummed paper each about 50 mm (2 in.) longer than the board.
2 Put some cold water in the bath and float the piece of paper in it for two or three minutes, pushing it beneath the surface of the water to ensure that it all gets completely wetted.

3 Lift out the paper by the two corners and drain off the excess water.

4 Lay the paper carefully on the board being careful not to crease it and making sure that a margin is left all round.

5 Damp a strip of the gummed paper by pulling it between the very damp cloth and the edge of a table.

6 Place the gum strip on the edge of the paper and rub it down with the damp cloth.

7 Repeat this on all sides and then stand the board up to dry naturally, well away from artificial heat, or the paper will split.

36 Materials needed for stretching paper

38 Draining the paper

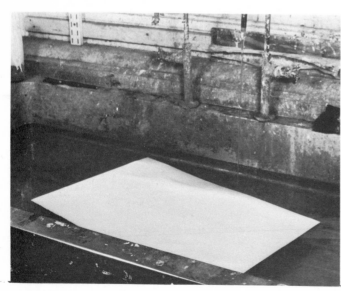

37 Soaking the sheet of paper

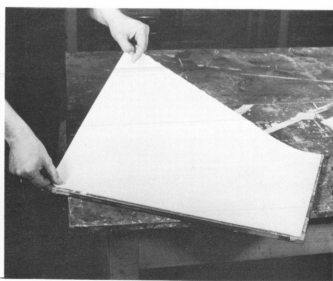

39 Laying the dampened paper on the board

40   Damping the gum strip

41   Sticking the paper to the board with gum strip

42   The paper stretched and ready for painting

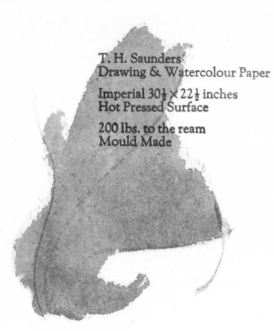

T. H. Saunders
Drawing & Watercolour Paper

Imperial 30½ × 22½ inches
Hot Pressed Surface

200 lbs. to the ream
Mould Made

T. H. Saunders
Drawing & Watercolour Paper

Imperial 30½ × 22½ inches
Rough Surface

200 lbs. to the ream
Mould Made

T. H. Saunders
Drawing & Watercolour Paper

Imperial 30½ × 22½ inches
Not Surface

200 lbs. to the ream
Mould Made

43 *Hot pressure surface*
Means that the paper is quite smooth but will hold a wash and accept pencil easily

44 *Not surface*
As its name implies it is not as smooth as hot pressed

45 *Rough surface*
A very heavy grained paper which is good for heavy washes but not very sympathetic to pencil or pen

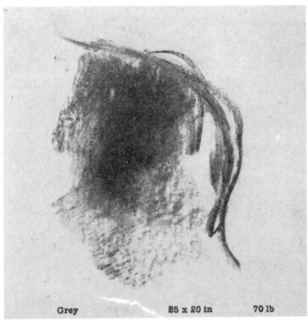

Grey   25 x 20 in   70 lb

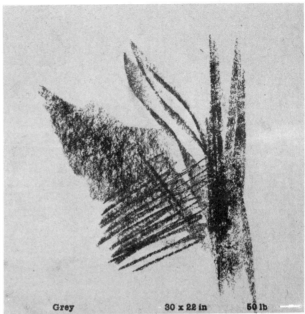

Grey   30 x 22 in   50 lb

Dark Green   30 x 22 in   48 lb

46 and 47   *Sugar papers*
Not suitable for painting as they are too absorbent and break up after a couple of applications of wash, but they are good as supports for charcoal and chalk drawings, and even the 70 lb weight paper is inexpensive

48   *Herga pastel paper*
A good paper made and sold especially for pastel work, available in nine colours and good to work on if you do not attempt to lay watercolour washes on it

The weight of the paper is an indication of the thickness. 200 lb to the ream means that the paper is very thick indeed.

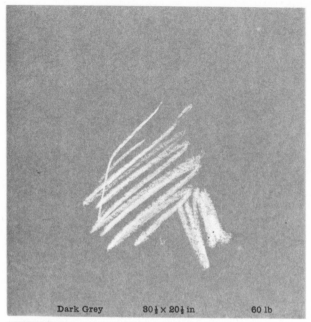

Dark Grey   30½ × 20½ in   60 lb

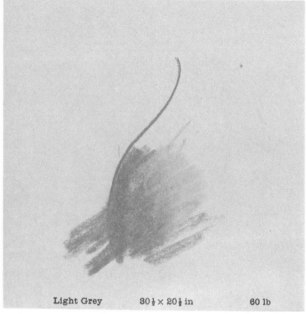

Light Grey   30½ × 20½ in   60 lb

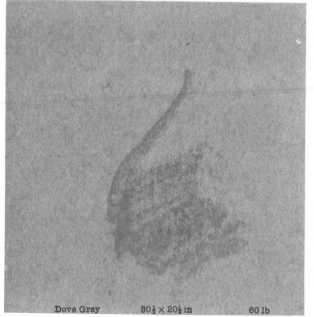

Dove Grey   30½ × 20½ in   60 lb

49 and 50   *Art Drawing paper*
A range of twelve colours from black to white, all of reasonable
quality but better used with pencil, pen and pastel than watercolour
unless stretched

51   *Bricol paper*
Again a range of twelve colours but not really much use as a support
for watercolour

Mist

Sand

52 and 53 *Ingres paper*
A beautiful paper with a slight tooth which takes watercolour, pencil or pastel without any difficulty. Sold in a range of twelve subtle tints

54 *Cartridge paper*
Many grades of cartridge paper are sold for drawing. Engineers quality 90 lb weight is probably one of the best but even this should be stretched before using watercolour on it

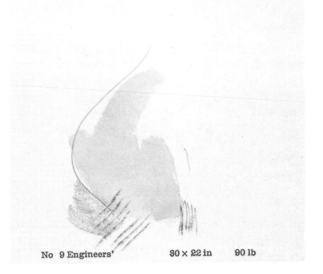

No 9 Engineers'   30 × 22 in   90 lb

Inks and liquid watercolours

Pen and wash is one of the oldest of the drawing techniques used by the artist. The linear composition drawn in ink and the tonal values added by using diluted washes.

Inks

Purely monochromatic drawings are generally made in sepia or black ink or sometimes a mixture of the two, using the diluted ink for the washes. Again all artist's suppliers sell drawing inks and one grows accustomed to one in preference to another. I like Chinese black ink; if the art store does not stock it try the local Chinese delicatessen who usually carry sticks of ink and also Chinese drawing brushes.

When diluting drawing inks, especially the coloured ones, there is a tendency with many of them for the colour to separate out into small granular marks. This can be partially prevented by using distilled water instead of tap water.

The colouring matter in many of the inks are dyes and they tend not to be light fast. It is therefore not advisable to paint in coloured inks if any degree of permanence is required.

The American firm of Stieg make a large range of what they call liquid watercolours in dropper bottles. Most of the colours are fugitive but some they guarantee to be reasonably light fast, at least enough to form a fair palette of colours. The colours are very concentrated and very pleasing to work with.

Pens

Personal preference is the only criteria here. There are a whole range of pens from mapping pens to pieces of stick. What is really needed is a drawing tip which is flexible and sympathetic to the way the artist works, and a means of holding enough ink in the pen so that one is not continually dipping it into the ink pot.

55 Wet paint into wet paint

56 Dragging paint with a dry brush

57 Wash over wax crayon

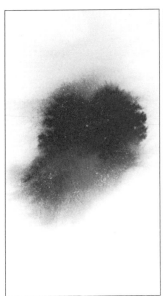

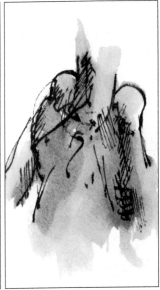

58 Wash on wet paper

59 Wash sponged out

60 Pencil into wet wash

61 Wash over ink

Types of pen

1 An ordinary pen nib in a holder with a detachable reservoir fitted on it is quite efficient because it can be filled with ink from a bottle with a dropper top.

2 *Rapidograph* pens and other stylographic pens are used widely and it is simple to change heads but they have the disadvantage of always producing the same thickness of line.

3 A cheap fountain pen with changeable screw-in nibs, such as the *Osmiroid* pen, is really a very attractive drawing instrument because nibs come in a very wide range and they are incredibly cheap to replace. They actually make a 'sketching pen' for artists.

4 A bamboo pen cut from a garden cane is a very good drawing instrument. The quality of mark it can make is better, in my opinion, than any other pen.

5 Felt-tipped pens are convenient but one can never be quite sure of the quality of mark that they are going to make. The tip invariably blunts after using a few times.

6 Nylon-tipped pens suffer from the same defects as felt-tipped pens. There are hundreds on the market. The best one I have found up to now is a Japanese pen called *Toughpoint*—the tip remains firm right up to the last mark.

7 Ball-point pens have never really been used as a drawing instrument. There is something about the way the ball slides on the surface of the paper and the sameness of the mark which makes them unsympathetic and difficult to control.

8 Goose-quill pens are very pleasant to work with. Collect half a dozen from the local poultry shop. Cut them on the slant and then split the tip of the pen. They eventually soften with continual use but when they do they can be recut easily.

62 Washes of waterproof ink on board. Note how the pigment ▶ has granulated in the right-hand corner

63   Soft layout pencil

65   Felt-tipped pen

67   Carbon pencil

64   Conte crayon

66   Pastel

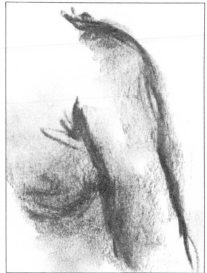

68   Charcoal

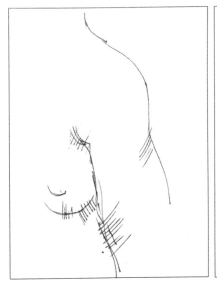

69 Nylon-tipped pen

71 HB lead pencil

73 Pastel pencil

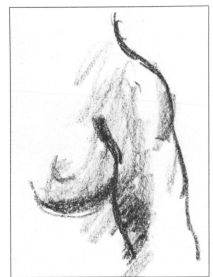

70 Wax crayon

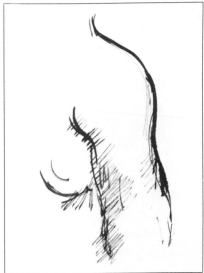

72 Goose quill

74 Bamboo

45

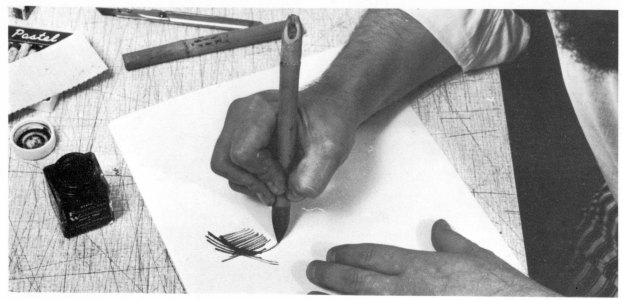

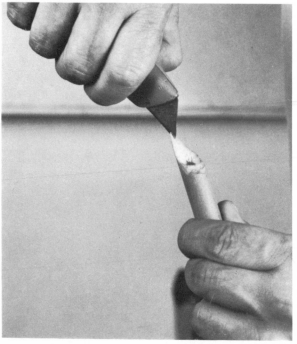

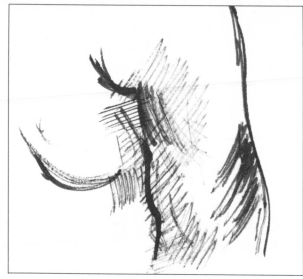

75 Drawing with the bamboo pen
76 Cutting a pen from a bamboo cane. Note that it is a fat cane
77 Bamboo pen and indian ink

78 Bamboo pen and liquid watercolour ▶

79 Drawing with a goose quill

80 Goose quill and indian ink

81 Cutting a pen from a goose quill. The same quill can be recut many times

Plate 3 *Apples, a bottle and the back of a chair by* Cézanne
Courtauld Institute Galleries
The strength of Cézanne's watercolour technique is shown brilliantly in this large still life painting. The controlled composition is never allowed to weaken, and the washes of closely related colours retain their brilliance and freshness throughout the painting

82 Quill pen drawing
with wash

83 *The Garden of Eden* by John Martin
The Tate Gallery, London
A sepia painting. The meticulous blobbing technique gives it a very
strange feeling indeed

84 *Tour d'Horloge*, Rouen, by David Cox
Pencil and wash. Pencil has been used to define all the detail and
the wash has been flooded in wet on wet in a very free way

Overleaf
85 Pen and coloured waterproof inks

86 *The Simoniac Pope* by William Blake
Pen and wash. Blake was primarily a draughtsman and the strong
linear quality is evident in all his work. This drawing was first made
in pencil then strengthened with pen and blue and red washes have
been used tonally

50

HELL
Canto 19

Pastel

Work executed in pastel is always referred to as 'pastel painting' although strictly it is a dry drawing technique blending colours on the paper itself.

Types

Traditionally pastels are sticks of dry pigment bound together by gum—usually gum tragacanth. The large range of subtle colours is obtained by extending the pure pigments with chalk. Messy to make in the studio and really not worth the trouble because crude pastels are cheap to buy, and artists' fine pastels are better than any one can make oneself.

There are literally dozens of proprietary makes on the market, ranging from the very cheap packets intended for children's use, to the beautiful soft artists' pastels that come in wooden cabinets.

The most expensive pastels are not only the softest but have the greatest range of colours. French and English manufacturers are reputed to make the best but the Japanese and the Germans make pastels of very high quality. Swann, a German company, markets a pastel pencil under the name *Othello* with a very wide range of colours and nowadays almost all manufacturers market an oil pastel. These are relatively cheap and blend well on paper, and if used in conjunction with turpentine they can be made to behave somewhat like watercolour washes.

Papers

Because of the nature of pastels it is as a rule best not to draw on very rough paper. There are a number of papers on the market specially made for drawing in pastel and these are usually tinted grey, brown or blue, about 48 lb weight. A slightly tinted paper is not a bad idea at all. Pastel being opaque does not need the reflective quality of the paper as does watercolour and the neutral tint of colour makes it easier to establish tonal and colour relationships at the beginning of work.

Recipe for a pastel ground

This is a recipe I found for putting a tooth onto cheap smooth paper thereby making it suitable for pastel work. It is not difficult to make and has a pleasing quality.

Method

1   Stretch paper in the way shown on page 34.

2   When it is dry and stretched, make up a starch solution by adding 1 part of vegetable starch (flour will do) to 3 parts of cold water, stirring into a smooth paste. Slowly add the paste to 3 parts of boiling water, stirring all the time. Allow to cool.

3   Add a little more water to the solution if necessary and then work into the paper with the bare hand or a sponge.

4   Sprinkle with powdered pumice to well cover the paper.

5   When dry, brush off all the surplus pumice and the ground is ready for drawing with pastel.

Fixatives

Pastel work needs fixing if it is to remain in good condition but it is also useful to partially fix bits of the drawing as one works to prevent smudging, or if a lot of overworking is to be done.

Fixative can be bought in bottles or spray guns from any art store. It is, however, possible to make a fixative for a fraction of the price. Here are some recipes.

Recipe No. 1

1 pt of alcohol (methylated spirit)
$\frac{1}{4}$ oz of white *shellac*.

Put the *shellac* into the bottle of alcohol and shake vigorously every day for a week or until the shellac has completely dissolved. The liquid should be slightly sticky to the touch, if it is not add more *shellac*. The mixture will not be com-pletely transparent, more of a milky colour, but when it is sprayed onto a pastel drawing the slight discoloration is not apparent.

Recipe No. 2

Into 1 pt of acetone dissolve as much celluloid as you can. Remove the emulsion from old nega-tive by soaking them in hot water, dry them, then push the celluloid into the bottle, screw the cap on and shake. Keep adding celluloid throughout a week or until the acetone will not take any more. Be careful with the mixture because ace-tone is powerful stuff.

Of the two recipes, I prefer the first one which works perfectly well, is cheaper and has a pleasant smell; in a closed room acetone is a little overpowering.

Recipe No. 3

Remove the skin of an egg yolk as shown in figure 112 and add 30 parts of water to the yolk liquid. Shake well in a bottle and spray on your drawing with a diffuser.

Recipe No. 4

Skim milk
Spray the work lightly with skim milk. This will in effect put a protective coat of casein over it.

Tools

Fingers are, of course, the most useful tools for blending and working in pastel colours, but for more exact blending there are stumps. These are made of soft paper rolled very tightly and give one a soft point which can be reformed time and time again. The stumps are sold in art stores, usually in bundles of a dozen.

Cotton buds, such as those used for cleaning babies' ears, are also useful tools for manipulat-ing pastel. These are especially good when using turpentine to work oil pastel because they hold quite an appreciable amount of turpentine.

87 Using a cotton bud dipped in turpentine to get a wash effect
with oil pastels

88–90 Oil pastels worked with turpentine and cotton buds

57

◀ 91 *Girl Reading a Newspaper* by Anquetin
The Tate Gallery, London
A beautiful example of pastel used by a master. The drawing has
a superb quality
Copyright SPADEM Paris

92 *Woman at her Toilet* by Degas
The Tate Gallery, London
Pastel at its best, used in a loose expressive way, left alone and not
overworked once the statement has been made

59

94 *Two Seated Figures* by Henry Moore
The Tate Gallery, London
Mixed media. Pen and chalk drawing with areas of wax to repel
the subsequent watercolour wash

◀ 93 *Horse and Rider* by Marino Marini
The Tate Gallery, London
Drawn in ink and pastel. The vigour of the pen drawing suggests
that he might have used a pen cut from a cane

95 *Somerset Place, Bath* by John Piper
The Tate Gallery, London
A painting in mixed media; pen, wash and pastel. John Piper's
rather theatrical technique is ideally suited to the paintings of
bombed buildings he made during the war

96 *A Classical Capriccio* by Robert Adam ▶
Sir John Soane's Museum
Adam the architect had a sensitive touch when he worked in
watercolour

62

97–100 Sketches for oil paintings made with *Othello* pastel pencils

◀ Plate 4 *Snowy Owl* by Barry Driscoll
Opaque underpainting of gouache over-glazed with transparent watercolour

65

101 Using a stub to work pastel on paper

102 Pastel used in conjunction with a stub in order to completely ▶
blend all the colours together

Tempera

Tempera is, to my mind, a watercolour technique rather than an oil painting technique. Tubes of *Tempera colour* can be bought from artists' suppliers and these colours lay very well on paper or board, but never give you the quality and brilliance of true egg tempera painted on a gesso ground.

Gesso ground

A gesso ground is just a chalk ground and is very easy to prepare and lay. Its main disadvantage is that it must be laid on a completely inert support otherwise it will crack. Seasoned wood, marine plywood or thick hardboard can all be used as supports. The size of the support must be kept small otherwise the gesso will pull and warp the support causing the ground to crack. Anything over 300 mm (12 in.) in either dimension must be cradled by sticking or screwing slats of wood onto the back of the support.

Method of preparation

1   It is always best to prepare half a dozen boards at a time so first cut hardboard or plywood to the sizes you want.

2   Prepare a strong size mixture and size both sides of the boards—allow to dry.

3   Using the warm gesso mixture brush the board in one direction only. Allow to dry and repeat, brushing in the other direction and then once more in the original direction.

4   When completely dry rub the surface down with No. 1 glasspaper to flatten the ridges left by the brush marks.

5   Lay three more coats of gesso, in the same way as No. 3.

6   Rub down with No. 0 glasspaper.

7   Three more coats of gesso and then rub down with flourpaper, which is the finest of the abrasive papers and should leave a beautiful smooth surface ready for painting.

It is a boring process preparing tempera boards but there is great satisfaction in preparing a perfect surface for painting and watching it gradually develop its pristine quality. If one doesn't paint on this surface, the whole quality of tempera is lost—which is the fantastic luminosity of the colours.

One word of warning—do not rush the preparation of the panels or air bubbles tend to appear in the gesso ground which when rubbed down with glasspaper reveal themselves as pin holes in the surface of the ground.

Gesso ground

Recipe

1 × 7 glue size mixture	1 pbm
Chalk	$\frac{1}{2}$ pbm
Zinc white	$\frac{1}{2}$ pbm

Method

Sieve the dry pigments into a little of the hot size until a thick smooth paste is made and then add the remainder of the size mixture—keep warm in a double boiler whilst making and applying.

Glue size under priming

Recipe

Commercial glue size	1 pbm
Water	7 pbm

Method

Put a little cold water in a suitable can and sprinkle on the powdered glue size, stirring all the time. As the granules of the glue swell add more water until a smooth paste forms. Then either make up with very hot water or add the remainder of the water cold and heat gently until all the size is dissolved, stirring all the time. DO NOT BOIL—boiling denatures size and destroys its adhesive and glutinous qualities. It should be brushed on hot and when cold should set into a loose jelly which will keep for several days.

½ P.B.M.   ½ P.B.M.

103 Material necessary for a gesso ground. 7:1 glue size mixture, chalk and zinc white

104 Sieving the dry materials into the size mixture

105 Force the powdered chalk and zinc white through the sieve with your fingers

106 Brushing the hot gesso ground

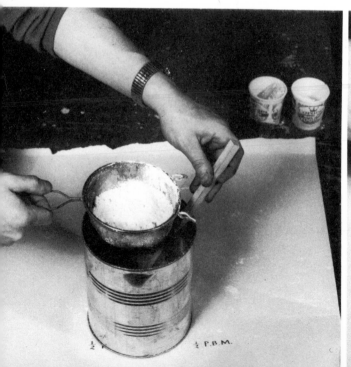

½   ½ P.B.M.

107   Materials and equipment necessary for making size

109   Sprinkling powdered size onto cold water

108   Making up the solution with hot water

Medium

The medium for tempera painting is egg yolk which is a natural emulsion. Its composition is generally given as

Water	51·5%	Lecithin	9·0%
Albumen	15·0%	Mineral matter	1·0%
Fat or oil	22·0%	Other substances	1·5%

Method

The lecithin is a fatty substance which is also hygroscopic and would appear to be the emulsifying agent in the egg yolk. The medium dries first by evaporation of the water and later by the drying of the oil to form a hard brilliant surface.

Once the yolk has been separated from the white (see figures 110 to 113) and a little water added, about half as much again, you are in business.

The medium can be added to raw pigments which have been ground in a little water or ready prepared tempera colours, gouache colours, designers colours or tubed watercolours can be used. It is easier to use already ground and bound colours and I tend to use designers colours for painting—this is not pure tempera painting I know, but then none of my paintings have ever cracked or fallen off their support.

If the medium is to be kept for a couple of days, add one drop of formaldehyde to the jar before closing it. However, take warning, it smells very strong indeed and eggs are really cheap enough to use a fresh one every day.

Painting

Method

1 Either draw directly on the board very lightly with pencil, or transfer your design by rubbing the back of the original drawing with brown conte crayon and then placing it on the board and tracing off with a blunt point like the end of a brush.

2 I suggest that the first paint applied should be kept as thin and washy as possible. Just take a little colour, a little egg medium and a good deal of water as if laying a watercolour wash, and just tint areas of the painting.

3 Having established the main areas of colour by means of thin wash—here the technique changes drastically from that of watercolour; one still paints from light to dark but the medium will not allow areas to be easily flooded with colour, so that one tends to use smallish brushes and a type of stippling technique. (Figure 116.)

4 The quality of the paint which is building up is one of fantastic luminosity—this can only be maintained if the colours are kept transparent, once white is added the opaque paint starts to kill the brilliance.

110   Breaking the egg

111   Isolating the yolk

112   Cutting the skin of the egg yolk

113   Releasing the egg yolk into the container whilst holding the skin

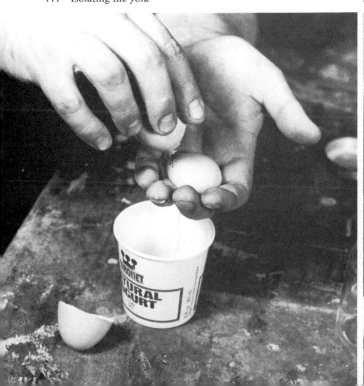

114 Egg tempera on a gesso ground. The first washes of colour laid on the light pencil drawing to indicate the basic areas of tone and colour

115 Egg tempera on a gesso ground. The second stage of a painting showing the build-up of washes of transparent colour and a
gradual strengthening of the form by means of more detailed
drawing with the brush

116 Egg tempera on a gesso ground. A more developed stage of a painting. The semi-stippling brush technique is evident and together with loose washes of transparent colour, well diluted with egg, the essential richness of the medium becomes apparent

117–119 Egg tempera on a gesso ground

120 *Edinburgh Castle* by Paul Sandby
The Tate Gallery, London
An example of a gouache technique, the painting is made completely in body colour

121 *Greyhound* by Barry Driscoll
Painted on watercolour board in commercial tempera colours and
watercolour. The incredible accuracy and detail of Barry Driscoll's
painting must make him one of the most outstanding of animal
painters alive today

Acrylic paints

I suppose that when oil painting on canvas was a new discovery old tempera painters shook their heads and said 'It will never catch on'. So the controversy moves around polyvinyl emulsions.

The thing is that being water soluble they can be manipulated as oil paint, or in the same manner as watercolour.

Used like oil paint, acrylic paints have a rather strange consistency and really are best when they are used to bind natural materials such as sand in the way in which the Spanish painter Tapies uses them.

At the other end of the scale they have the advantage over ordinary watercolour in that each wash of colour becomes permanent and waterproof and therefore will not lift off when overpainted. This is a considerable advantage and some artists have evolved particular techniques based on this fact.

Barry Evans, the illustrator, uses acrylic designers colours on a silk screen printing board called *malex* board, which is a very thick smooth surfaced white board. He first lays on a smooth wet wash over the whole surface and then picks it off by pressing pieces of non-absorbent lithographic proofing paper on to the work (figures 122 to 127). Further washes of different transparent colour are laid on and pulled off in the same way until the picture starts to suggest its form—then parts of the picture are painted out and others delineated until the whole thing takes shape.

In the hands of an expert this technique is a joy to watch and incredibly accurate and variable. In the hands of an amateur it is not at all accurate but as a stimulus to the imagination cannot be beaten even though it can be wasteful of materials.

122   Putting the first wash of acrylic designers' colour onto *malex* board

123   Blotting the wash of colour with non-absorbent paper

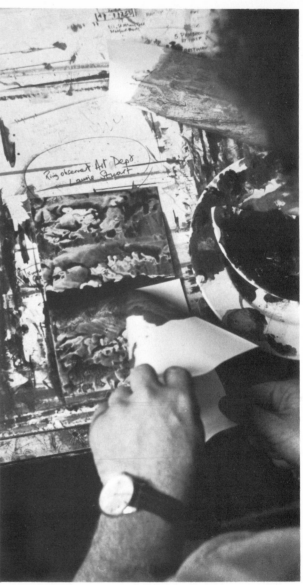

124   Added washes being worked in a different way with a piece of cardboard

125   Third wash of colour being manipulated with paper

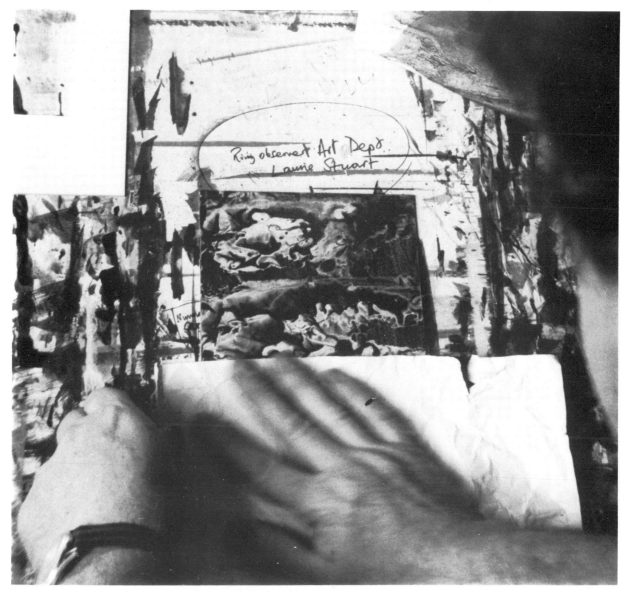

126 Using crumbled paper to make different marks in the wet paint

Overleaf
127 The beginning of a landscape now ready for masking and development in any way the artist wishes

128–130 Progressive examples of the painting technique

131   Detail from *The Death of Shakespeare* by Barry Evans
Acrylic designers' colour on *malex* board. The figures have been
painted in opaque body colour but wherever possible the artist has
left the original paint quality of the preliminary washes to show
through, as for example in the cloak of the old man and the mantle
surrounding the girl

132   Detail from a painting by Barry Evans showing the use of ▶
over-painting on the original transparent washes

133 *Magical Landscape by* Barry Evans
From the collection of A. J. F. Hitchins
A typical painting by this artist who finds his painting in the
preliminary washes of acrylic colour which he manipulates on the
board before painting out areas and developing them with body
colour

134 and 135   Details of *Magical Landscape* ▶

136   *Head* by Barry Evans
Acrylic designers' colours painted in the manner described on
page 80

▶

137 *The Jester by* Barry Evans
Painted on board in acrylic designers' colours

138 *The Queen and Her Keeper* by Barry Evans
Acrylic designers' colour and body colour painted on board

Suppliers

Great Britain

Artists' materials of all kinds
E J Arnold (*School Suppliers*)
Butterley Street
Leeds LS10 1AX

Dryad (*Reeves*) *Limited*
Northgates
Leicester LE1 4QR

L. Cornelissen and Sons
22 Great Queen Street
London WC2

Lechertier Barbe Limited
95 Jermyn Street
London SW1

Clifford Milburn Limited
54 Fleet Street
London EC4

Reeves and Sons Limited
Lincoln Road
Enfield
Middlesex

C. Robersons and Company Limited
71 Parkway
London NW1

George Rowney and Company Limited
10 Percy Street
London W1

Winsor and Newton Limited
51 Rathbone Place
London W1

Shellac is obtainable from almost
every Do It Yourself shop and from
hardware store.

Suppliers
United States

Artists materials of all kinds

Arthur Brown and Bro. Inc
2 West 46 Street
New York, NY 10036

Grumbacher
460 West 34 Street
New York

A. I. Friedman Inc
25 West 45 Street
New York, NY 10036

The Morilla Company Inc
43 21st Street, Long Island City
New York and
2866 West 7 Street
Los Angeles, California

New Masters Art Division

California Products Corporation
169 Waverley Street
Cambridge, Massachusetts

Permanent Pigments
Cincinnati, Ohio

Shiva Products
Paducah, Kentucky

Stafford-Reeves Inc
626 Greenwich Street
New York, NY 10014

Steig Products
PO Box 19, Lakewood
New Jersey 08701

Winsor and Newton Inc
555 Winsor Drive
Secaucus, New Jersey 07094